THE
PATH

ANXIETY & PANIC ATTACK ELIMINATION PROGRAM

Miller Thomson

Copyright 2018 Miller Thomson

All rights reserved

CONTENTS

INTRODUCTION 1

CHAPTER 1 12

SELF-RATING ANXIETY SCALE 12

CHAPTER 2 23

PANIC ATTACK FIRST AID KIT 23

    2.1. BREATHING EXERCISES 28

    2.2. PROGRESSIVE MUSCLE RELAXATION 34

CHAPTER 3 42

ANTI-ANXIETY DIET 42

    3.1. WHAT TO AVOID 46

    3.2. WHAT TO USE 56

CHAPTER 4 65

HABITS 65

- 4.1. EATING AND DRINKING HEALTHY 68
- 4.2. SMILING 70
- 4.3. SLEEPING 73
- 4.4. EXERCISE 81
- 4.5. QUIT SMOKING 87

CHAPTER 5 92

SETTING GOALS 92

CHAPTER 6 101

PERCEPTION FALLACIES 101

- 6.1. FILTERING 105
- 6.2. CATASTROPHIZING 107
- 6.3. BLACK AND WHITE THINKING 110
- 6.4. JUMPING TO CONCLUSIONS 112
- 6.5. OVERGENERALI- 114
- ZATION 114
- 6.6. MISLABELING 117
- 6.7. ALWAYS BEING RIGHT 119
- 6.8. BLAMING 121
- 6.9. PERSONALIZATION 123

- 6.10. CONTROL FALLACY 125
- 6.11. EMOTIONAL REASONING 127
- 6.12. FALLACY OF FAIRNESS 129
- 6.13. FALLACY OF CHANGE 131
- 6.14. SHOULDS 133
- 6.15. HEAVEN'S REWARD FALLACY 135

CHAPTER 7 139

7 STEPS TO ELIMINATE ANXIETY 139

- 7.1. JOURNALING 142
- 7.2. IDENTIFYING FALLACIES 147
- 7.3. THOUGHT RESTRUCTURING 150
  - 7.3.1. NOTICE POSITIVES 158
- 7.4. ON-THE-SPOT THOUGHT RESTRUCTURING 161
- 7.5. GOING ALL THE WAY 166
- 7.6. EXPOSURE 170
- 7.7. WELCOMING ANXIETY 175

CHAPTER 8 181

SPECIFIC FEARS 181

- 8.1. FEAR OF PUBLIC SPEAKING 184

8.2. FEAR OF FLYING 190

8.3. FEAR OF HEIGHTS 194

CONCLUSION 197

INTRODUCTION

On my journey to rediscover my cool, calm and collected self again I was shocked to discover how much of the material out there is nothing more than wishful thinking. I already had to deal with people in my life who did not understand what I am going through. Paying money, spending time and energy to read a book just to get an advice of "just wish it away" was insulting.

This is not one of those books. This book contains proven tools and techniques that employ short, middle and long term strategies to eliminate panic attacks and to reduce anxiety to normal level. I have been where you are now and I felt what you are feeling. This is why I want to help you to rediscover the old you.

Anxiety is so prevalent that it is hard to explain others what you feel. More often than not I would hit a wall of "Yeah, I had a hard day at work too" or "Just be positive." What you are feeling goes way beyond your usual everyday worries but how can you explain this to someone?

The worst thing anxiety can do to you is make you feel like you are completely alone. That sinking feeling that you can not explain what you feel or open up to anyone because they will not understand, locks you up in a prison of your own.

I wrote this book due to my own personal experience. My interest in anxiety and panic attacks stems from years of suffering. My personal and professional life was at a stand still as I was gripped by fear and worry. Breaking out of this prison took me years of studying and working on myself and due to that this is not an academic paper discussing advantages of certain technique. This is a program which combines techniques that work into a comprehensive system.

It is scary to open up and admit that what you are dealing with is more serious than what most people feel. You might even feel ashamed to have these feelings.

News are filled with stories about people who lost everything so you may even be talking down to yourself. You may be trying to get yourself "out of this funk" by blaming yourself. How can you allow yourself to feel this way when there are so many people who are much worse off.

You feel that you need to show your kids, colleagues, loved ones or employees that you are a strong person.

Do not allow such feelings to stop you from working on yourself and seeking help.

Having anxiety does not make you any less stronger. Everyone feels some level of anxiety and this experience does not mean that you are weak, it just means that you are a human.

You are not alone.

Reading these words is an important first step you take on your road to taking your life back. Once you regain your strength, your confidence and the joy of life, you can help others but for now you need to focus on yourself.

Share your experiences and feelings with people in your life. Even if you feel that right now you do not have anyone in your life you can open up to, there are people waiting to hear you out and help you . Call assistance phone numbers or chat in Internet forums. The most important thing is to get your issues out and maybe once they are out you will be able to review them from a different perspective and solution will present itself.

Opening up allows you to break out of that crushing feeling of loneliness. You will learn that others have their anxieties and worries too.

Every new day brings out many new challenges you need to face and obstacles you need to overcome. You may worry about money, health, relationships or you may suffer from specific anxiety like social anxiety, specific phobia, panic disorder, obsessive compulsive disorder or post-traumatic stress disorder.

Every single person experiences some level of anxiety every day. Anxiety is actually a very important mechanism that allows you to call upon additional strength reserves when you need them and to direct your focus on what is important.

That being said, every mechanism sometimes breaks down and anxiety becomes a crippling obstacle. Normal anxiety level gives you extra boost but severe anxiety locks you up and stops you from living a life you deserve.

Before we move forward with this program I have a very big favor to ask you regarding phones.

Please do not use your phone while reading and working with this book and while you are working on your exercises. If you can allow this, please turn off your phone and leave it in another room.

This will most likely initially cause you discomfort but please power through this. I am asking you this because phone is a source of constant distraction and one of the factors negatively impacting your anxiety level.

The first step you can take towards a reduction of your anxiety is to set a time during the day when you will turn your phone off . Preferably one hour before going to sleep.

If turning your phone off may be out of the question because you have kids or due to other circumstances, there is a solution. Use "do not disturb" app. These apps turn off all notifications and calls but allow you to set phone numbers that are not blocked. Let people know that they can reach you in case of an emergency but if it can wait, they should wait after your "no phone" period to contact you.

German car manufacturer Volkswagen signed an agreement with its employees which stipulates that once they are done for the day, employees can switch theirs phones off. This allows employees of this company to actually relax after work and forget about it. This significantly improved productivity as people are able to actually get real rest. This is why this policy has been employed by a number of other companies.

You may have not noticed it before but constant connectivity is a huge source of stress and anxiety. This connectivity erodes your personal space and significantly reduces your ability to disconnect from work and worries.

Making a commitment to introduce no-phone time signifies the start of the program as this is the first active step you are taking.

It is of utmost importance to figure out the level of anxiety you are experiencing right now, to know what you are dealing with. This is the reason why the next step in your journey towards taking back your life is an anxiety level test. Please fill in a quick questionnaire as this will allow you to better understand how severe your anxiety is.

This test will take only a few minutes to complete and it will be tremendously helpful. All you need is a pen and a calculator. Your phone calculator can be used for this purpose.

One of the most crippling afflictions a person can experience is a panic attack. Second chapter is Panic Attack First Aid Kit. This chapter introduces you to powerful breathing and muscle relaxation techniques which will allow you to stop panic attack in its tracks. The use of these techniques will help you relax and eliminate panic attacks from your life.

Severity of panic attacks necessitates that we address this issue head on and right away. If you are experiencing panic attacks, first we need to get this under control before you can move on to the long term anxiety management strategies covered in the following chapters.

I recommend you to read and practice these techniques even if you do not suffer from panic attacks as this chapter contains strategies that will help you stay cool, calm and collected even in highly stressful situations like public speaking, taking exam, flying and other stressful events.

This book will allow you to bring back the old you. Once again you will be able to travel, socialize, exercise, work and have fun with your friends and loved ones without a trace of worry or fear. Building confidence and leaving worry behind will allow you to reach new heights in your career, expand your business, travel, have fun, build strong and loving relationships.

Getting your anxiety under control will allow you to achieve things that right now you may think are out of your reach.

You deserve to experience life and everything it has to offer without worry and fear. With your determination and diligence this program will allow you to achieve happiness and peace of mind you deserve.

CHAPTER 1

SELF-RATING ANXIETY SCALE

You can deal with the problem only if you can understand it. In this chapter you will find Zung Self-Rating Anxiety Scale. We will be using this test due to its proven accuracy and ease of use. This test was developed by Williem W. K. Zung M.D. to quantify level of anxiety person is experiencing.

The Self-Rating Anxiety Scale measures anxiety level using 20 questions based on 4 groups of anxiety manifestations: cognitive, autonomic, motor and central nervous system symptoms. Please indicate how much each statement applies to you based on the previous two weeks.

Each answer is scaled from 1 to 4. Please read questions carefully as some of them are negatively worded as to prevent set response. To sum up your score use the scale, which you can find below the test.

Take a piece of paper and answer these questions selecting which applies to you best: A; B; C or D.

A - A little of the time

B - Some of the time

C - Good part of the time

D - Most of the time

1. I feel more nervous and anxious than usual.

2. I feel afraid for no reason at all.

3. I get upset easily or feel panicky.

4. I feel like I am falling apart and going to pieces.

5. I feel that everything is all right and nothing bad will happen.

6. My arms and legs shake and tremble.

7. I am bothered by headaches, neck and back pain.

8. I feel weak and get tired easily.

9. I feel calm and can sit still easily.

10. I can feel my heart beating fast.

11. I am bothered by dizzy spells.

12. I have fainting spells or feel like it.

13. I can breathe in and out easily.

14. I get numbness and tingling in my fingers and toes.

15. I am bothered by stomach aches or indigestion.

16. I have to empty my bladder often.

17. My hands are usually dry and warm.

18. My face gets hot and blushes.

19. I fall asleep easily and get a good night's rest.

20. I have nightmares.

You have your answers so it is time to tally your score. Please calculate your score using this answer key:

1. A - 1; B - 2; C - 3; D - 4
2. A - 1; B - 2; C - 3; D - 4
3. A - 1; B - 2; C - 3; D - 4
4. A - 1; B - 2; C - 3; D - 4
5. A - 4; B - 3; C - 2; D - 1
6. A - 1; B - 2; C - 3; D - 4
7. A - 1; B - 2; C - 3; D - 4
8. A - 1; B - 2; C - 3; D - 4
9. A - 4; B - 3; C - 2; D - 1
10. A - 1; B - 2; C - 3; D - 4
11. A - 1; B - 2; C - 3; D - 4
12. A - 1; B - 2; C - 3; D - 4
13. A - 4; B - 3; C - 2; D - 1
14. A - 1; B - 2; C - 3; D - 4
15. A - 1; B - 2; C - 3; D - 4
16. A - 1; B - 2; C - 3; D - 4
17. A - 4; B - 3; C - 2; D - 1
18. A - 1; B - 2; C - 3; D - 4

19. A - 4; B - 3; C - 2; D - 1
20. A - 1; B - 2; C - 3; D - 4

Calculate your score to find out your anxiety level:

20-44   Normal Range
45-59   Mild to Moderate Anxiety Levels
60-74   Marked to Severe Anxiety Levels
75-80   Extreme Anxiety Levels

Normal Range

If you scored up to 44 points that means that you experience low levels of anxiety. You may have felt inclined to read this book because you felt a sudden spike of anxiety. If this was caused by a specific event like, for example, an upcoming public speaking event, you can learn tactics that will help you deal with these specific issues. Breathing and muscle relaxation exercises will help you relieve stress.

Mild to Moderate Anxiety Level

If you scored in a range of 45 - 59 that means that you experience elevated levels of anxiety in your daily life. Some changes in your daily routine and your diet are required. Follow advice and exercises which are provided in this book to lower your anxiety level to a normal range.

Market to Severe Anxiety Level

If you scored in a range of 60 - 74 that means that your anxiety level is high. Dealing with anxiety has to be high priority for you. Follow this program with dedication and persistence and soon you will notice your anxiety level drop.

Extreme Anxiety Level

If you scored above 75 that means that you are suffering from extremely high levels of anxiety. This level of anxiety is accompanied by a severe form of anxiety - panic attack. In the next chapter you will learn breathing and muscle relaxation techniques that will help you stop panic attack in it's tracks and eliminate them from your life. With the help of exercises, diet and lifestyle changes you will be able to reduce your anxiety to a normal level.

IMPORTANT

If your symptoms are mostly physical make sure to complete a physical exam in order to rule out physical issues.

Do you experience these symptoms:

- Severe lack of energy or drive.
- Flat affect (complete lack of emotion) along with slowed thinking and behaviors.
- Severe appetite changes, headaches, and sleep problems.

If you feel these symptoms you may be experiencing depression and you need to consult your doctor. Please call and arrange a consultation with your doctor.

! If you experience suicidal thoughts please contact your doctor right away !

CHAPTER 2

PANIC ATTACK FIRST AID KIT

Panic attack is a sudden period of intense fear. Panic attacks are often accompanied by physical symptoms such as palpitation, sweating, shaking, shortness of breath, numbness and even chest pains.

These experiences can last anywhere from a few seconds to hours but the most important thing to take in is that PANIC ATTACKS ARE NOT PHYSICALLY DANGEROUS. Although it might not feel this way when you are experiencing one, those symptoms will pass.

The most important first step is to ensure your safety. Panic attacks can be triggered or occur unexpectedly and due to that you may find yourself in a dangerous situation when panic attack starts. Before you employ panic attack elimination techniques ensure that you are safe.

Panic attack may occur, for example, while you are driving. In this case you need to safely bring your vehicle to a stop and only after you have done that, start using techniques you will learn in this chapter. Even if you are late to an important meeting you have to stop what you are doing and take your time to employ these techniques.

First off, you need to understand what is happening.

Anxiety is not a disease. It is a normal mechanism that is given to us by nature in order to keep us alive. Movies might portray fearlessness as a desired trait but in real life being fearless means taking unnecessary risks.

Anxiety is like having a caring mother, who is reminding you to keep yourself safe and focus on important tasks. This is a normal to mild anxiety level or what may be called your normal everyday worries. Anxiety becomes an issue when it is moderate to extreme. Panic attack is an extreme manifestation of fear.

Panic attack is a fear of fear itself. This is why it is so disruptive and vicious. It is self sustaining and self amplifying. As frightening as a panic attack may seem you will learn how to stop it and in later chapters we will address underlying issues that cause your anxiety in the first place.

How do you stop a panic attack?

Breathing exercises and muscle relaxation exercises.

These exercises address physical symptoms of a panic attack so use these techniques in accordance to symptoms you experience during the attack.

If you feel shortness of breath, feeling of choking, palpitations and/or shortness of breath - it is best to use breathing exercises.

If your symptoms are trembling and shaking, sweating, hot or cold flashes, nausea, chest pain and discomfort - use muscle relaxation exercises.

Panic attacks rarely have just one or two symptoms accompanying them. Choose technique you feel works the best. Once you have enough experience, employ both techniques at the same time as the use of them both at the same time amplifies their effectiveness.

2.1. BREATHING EXERCISES

Panic attack is a horrendous experience but it is not physically dangerous to you. One of the most discomforting types of symptoms is shortness of breath. You can feel that you just can not get any air inside your lungs. You can feel dizzy and think that you will suffocate, but you will not.

You will not suffocate during a panic attack.

This was the symptom I feared the most and as a result would get most often.

Panic attack is fear of fear itself and due to that you get what you fear the most.

Doctor David D. Burns has developed a very effective breathing exercise which disrupts the escalation of panic attack and stops it completely. This technique has been proven to be highly effective in terminating panic attacks as well as having a number of health benefits.

You may be tempted to use the paper bag technique we often see on TV. As many other things you see on TV - this technique is used by cinema and TV not due to its effectiveness but due to its visual properties.

It is much easier for the audience to understand that an actor is trying to deal with a panic attack if he or she is heavily breathing into a bag as compared to someone using measured breathing.

Measured breathing is a 5 - 2 - 5 technique which employs breathing using your diaphragm. It is very simple and easy to employ but for the first few times please practice it while you are in a calm state.

Usually when you breath you can feel your shoulders and chest rising. Follow these steps to learn diaphragmatic breathing:

1. Lie on your back on a flat surface (or in bed) with your knees bent. You can use a pillow under your head and your knees for support, if that is more comfortable.

2. Place one hand on your upper chest and the other on your belly, just below your rib cage.

3. Breathe in slowly through your nose, letting the air in deeply, towards your lower belly. The hand on your chest should remain still, while the one on your belly should rise.

4.   Tighten your abdominal muscles and let them fall inward as you exhale through pursed lips. The hand on your belly should move down to its original position.

You can also practice this sitting in a chair, with your knees bent and your shoulders, head, and neck relaxed. Do this until you get used to it.

Once you got used to diaphragmatic breathing it is time to practice measured breathing technique for stopping panic attacks. It simply adds one element to diaphragmatic breathing - counting.

1.   Breathe in through your nose for 5 seconds.

2.   Hold air in for 2 seconds.

3.   Slowly breathe out through your mouth for 5 seconds.

Repeat this process until you feel that your panic attack symptoms dissipated.

This exercise might sound deceptively simple but it actually has a number of positive effects that are extremely effective at stopping panic attacks.

First off, counting and concentrating on breathing distracts you. I learned the power of a distraction very early on. As a child I was terrified of needles. The idea of a needle penetrating my skin put me in a state of panic. Every time I had to have a shot, right before the doctor administered a shot, my dad would surprise me with a toy or a candy. I never felt those shots.

Second, diaphragmatic breathing stimulates release of serotonin - the happy chemical. This way diaphragmatic breathing reduces stress, improves digestion, sleep and mood.

Third, breath counting and steady pace of breathing reduces your heart rate and blood pressure.

Finally, diaphragmatic breathing exercises abdomen muscles and improves your posture.

Use this exercise on a regular basis to take advantage of these numerous advantages it has to offer.

2.2. PROGRESSIVE MUSCLE RELAXATION

Muscle relaxation exercises address muscle tension which is a common reaction to stress. These techniques can be especially helpful for panic attack elimination in that they provide a proactive way to assist in symptom management. This exercise requires at least 10 minutes. Even if you are working on a deadline you need to allow yourself minimum of 10 minutes.

Sometimes it feels like you can not spare even a minute but you have to. This will help you finish your tasks much faster. By taking this short time off you will win more time. Tired and stressed person works only at a fraction of her or his capability. We are also more prone to making mistakes in this state which adds to time task takes to finish.

You can allow and even have to take a short break, as it will help you regain your composure, as well as taking a break will help you work efficiently and avoid mistakes.

Progressive muscle relaxation involves tensing and relaxing the muscles in your body, one muscle group at a time. It can also reduce other reactions to stress, such as rapid breathing and heartbeat, stomach problems, and headache.

> **IMPORTANT**
>
> If you feel pain during this exercise - stop. Be aware of existing traumas and if you are not sure if it is safe to do any part of this exercise, do not try. In this case it is best to consult your doctor.

Follow these instructions:

1. Find a quiet, comfortable place. You can do this exercise in a chair or lying down.

2. Close your eyes, if you are comfortable doing so. However, if you have experienced traumatic stressors (such as serving in military combat or an assault), you may want to keep them open. This can help you stay "grounded" in the "here and now." Do what is most comfortable for you.

3. Take a few slow, deep breaths.

4. Inhale deeply through your nose with your mouth closed to a count of four.

5. Exhale through your mouth slowly - also to a count of four. On the exhale, imagine that the tension is leaving your body, flowing out with each exhale.

6. Repeat this three to four times. If at any point you feel dizzy or light-headed, return to your normal breathing.

7. Continue to breathe deeply as you move into the muscle tension and relaxation part of this exercise. You will begin with your feet and work your way up. As you inhale, tense and hold each muscle for a count of four. Relax that muscle group as you breathe out. Take several breaths before you move to the next part of your body. Allow some time to feel the relaxation.

8. Tense the muscles of your feet by pointing your toes and tightening your feet as you inhale. Hold this tension briefly, then relax your toes and feet as

you breathe out. Imagine the tension flowing out with your breath. Notice the difference between the tension and relaxation.

9. Press the balls of your feet into the floor and raise your heels, allowing your calf muscles to contract. Feel the tension in your calves for a moment. Then release and notice your muscles relax. Again, have the tension and relaxation match your breath. Tighten your knees and allow your legs to straighten. Feel the tightness in the front of your legs. Notice the sense of tension as you inhale. And release on the exhale, allowing your legs to bend and relax back onto the floor.

10. Squeeze the muscles of your buttocks. Notice the feeling of tension as you inhale. Hold this for just a moment. And on your exhale, release and allow your muscles to relax, letting the tension melt away.

11. Continue up through your body. Concentrate now on your stomach.

Contract your stomach and continue to breathe. Hold the tension for a count of four. Inhale deeply. As you exhale, let your stomach relax. Again, notice the difference between the tension and relaxation.

12. Move your attention now to your hands. Curl your fingers into a tight fist in each hand. Hold your fists tight and notice the sense of tension as you continue to breathe. As you release your fists, let your hands relax back to a natural position. And notice the difference between the feeling of tension and relaxation in your hands.

13. Bend both arms now at the elbow (like Popeye). Flex both of your arms by making fists and pulling your fists up tightly to your shoulders. Notice the feeling in the tensed muscles of your upper arms. Take another inhale and as you exhale and relax your arms down to your sides. Take notice of any change in

what you feel as you go from a state of tension to relaxation.

14. Push your shoulders up to your ears now. Hold this "shrugging" position for just a moment. Feel the tension in your neck and shoulder muscles. Feel the tension melt away as you relax your shoulders back down. Continue to breathe in and out.

15. Finish by tensing the muscles in your face. Scrunch your face as if you just bit into something sour. Feel your eyebrows pull together, your eyes pinch tightly shut, and your lips purse together. Notice the sensation of tenseness in your face for just a moment. Then allow your face to relax. Notice the release of tension from your forehead, eyes, cheeks, mouth and jaw.

16. See if you can find any other spot of tension in your body. Notice it and let it go.

17. Let yourself be still for a few moments. Just experience your relaxed muscles. Continue to breathe slowly and deeply. Feel any tension flow out. Your relaxation can get deeper with each breath.

18. When you are ready, bring your attention back to your breathing. Notice your body and how it feels. If you have had your eyes closed, imagine the room. When you are ready, open your eyes.

Among others, this exercise is employed by the U.S. Department of Veterans Affairs to help veterans deal with such traumatic experiences as battle fatigue and post-traumatic stress disorder. Progressive muscle relaxation stops your panic attack on multiple levels by providing distraction, eliminating physical symptoms and by improving your health.

Practice for a few times in a calm state to get to know this exercise and to learn its steps. This exercise can be used in combination with measured breathing to utilize the amplifying effect to increase effectiveness of them both.

CHAPTER 3

ANTI-ANXIETY DIET

Food and drinks are our fuel. Things you eat and drink have a significant and direct impact on how you feel. Hippocrates noted important role food plays in the state of your health, *"Let food be thy medicine and medicine be thy food."*

If you put the wrong gas into a car it will break. We are much more complicated and finely tuned systems than machines so it is no wonder that our "fuel" has even more important role on how we feel and perform.

I will be honest with you - information you will discover below will require you to make changes to your daily habits. This will take some getting used to and will require some effort on your parts.

Do you want to live without anxiety hanging over you like a storm cloud?

Do you want to be happy?

Do you want to achieve success in your professional life?

Do you want to have fun with your friends and to build loving relationships?

Answering yes to these questions means that you are ready to take action. You have to make a commitment right now. Doing the same thing can result only in the same outcome so it is time for a change.

The way you feel greatly depends on the state of your health. Your goal is to live a happy life without panic attacks and anxiety. Achievement of this goal will require you to stop eating products that are bad for you and have been proven to heighten anxiety. You have to adapt necessary changes to rediscover happiness, strength and confidence.

This is not the time for half-measures. A plane can not fly if it has parts missing. Lifestyle changes you will find below are an essential part of panic attack elimination and anxiety management process, which are essential to ensure the success.

3.1. WHAT TO AVOID

More often than not we take food for granted and view it simply as fuel we need to consume in order to be able to function. With the attitude like that it is no wonder that our diets become dominated by unhealthy products as they are widely available and require little to no effort on our part.

Improving your life means "opening your eyes" and selecting things that are beneficial to you and avoiding things that drag you down. When it comes to food and beverages there are three items that are working against you. Unfortunately all of them are very addictive so you need to be strong and getting rid of them will require ingenuity and determination.

These three items are caffeine, alcohol and processed foods.

Naturally some things are worse than others so if you can not imagine your day without a cup of coffee or two do not despair.

You do not have to eliminate caffeine from your life completely. Caffeine itself is not bad for you. The damage is caused by excessive consumption of coffee and especially energy drinks. You need to monitor and reduce your intake if necessary, but you do not have to cut coffee from your life completely.

Recommended daily maximum intake is actually pretty high and stands at 300 mg. To give you some context one Starbucks espresso shot contains roughly

80 mg and a cup of filtered coffee is 70 - 130 mg. One cup of strong black tea is around 70 mg of caffeine. You can treat yourself to few cups a day for when you need that extra energy boost.

That being said, you need to make adjustments to the way you are getting your caffeine. If you prefer drinking coffee without "upgrades" or you enjoy drinking unsweetened tea- you are in the clear. Problem is various "frappuccinos" and energy drinks.

You need to stop drinking energy drinks. Period. No more energy drinks.

Studies have shown that caffeine is the least of your worries when it comes to energy drinks. Study conducted by Sachin A. Shah of David Grant Medical Center on Travis Air Force Base and University of the Pacific in Stockton, California revealed that energy drinks caused heartbeat irregularities and spikes in blood pressure.

These results were not observed in control groups who consumed only caffeine containing drinks. Heartbeat irregularity and blood pressure spikes can be attributed to a large quantity of sugar, several B vitamins, taurine and other ingredients which are present in energy drinks.

Similarly coffee drinks should be avoided not due to caffeine they contain but due to other various ingredients. Usually these coffee drinks contain only one shot of espresso so they are way below daily caffeine limit. The danger lies in an extremely high amounts of sugar and other additives. These drinks also have an extremely high calorie count. Some of those "frappuccinos" come close to or even exceed calorie count of Big Mac.

Keep in mind that you need to monitor when you drink your coffee or tea. It is recommended to avoid caffeine after six o'clock as it might have adverse effect on your ability to fall asleep. Another reason to stay away from caffeine after six is nightmares. Because caffeine is a powerful psychoactive drug, caffeine directly stimulates brain activity, even during sleep, which can lead to nightmares.

Processed foods are the second class of products you need to avoid. Unlike caffeine, you should abstain from processed foods completely.

Processed foods encompasses such food categories as fast food, ready-to-eat meals, snacks, cakes and cookies. Processed foods are extremely convenient at a cost of being bad for you. Movie Fast Food Nation explores this issue and Eric Schlosser noted, *"Fast food is popular because it is convenient, it is cheap, and it tastes good. But the real cost of eating fast food never appears on the menu."*

During the manufacture process ingredients are sterilized and undergo other manipulations stripping ingredients of their nutritional value and completely destroying their taste and texture. To make this food suitable for consumption large quantities of sugar, salt and other additives are added. Take away these additives and you will end up with a discolored, tasteless pile of thing that barely resembles food.

I understand that it is extremely hard to find necessary time to prepare food from scratch. It is very hard until you will get into the habit of doing it and gather necessary ingredients. Search YouTube and you will find endless supply of healthy recipes that take less than 20 minutes to prepare.

To make the process even faster, during workdays I prepare large portion for lunch and next days dinner. To add a bit of variety to the taste simply add different spices. This way preparation of healthy food takes no longer than to cook frozen pizza as you are making two meals at the same time.

Consumption of processed foods is usually the hardest thing to let go but you need to eliminate these products from your life if you want to eliminate panic attacks and get your anxiety to a normal level. This action requires determination and vigilance.

Processed foods have been getting a lot of bad press and manufacturers are fighting back with deception. They use healthy sounding product names, insert various sentences that refer to freshness or healthiness of the product and even use rigged studies to base their bogus health claims on their packaging.

Although Natural American Spirit is not food, but it is a great example of these deception tactics at work. These cigarettes are made on the same production lines using the same ingredients as any other brand. They are not in any way healthier. The only difference is the name.

Everything is made so you would not think that this is the same cancer stick as any other brand and it worked. In a national survey of smokers, almost 64 percent of Natural American Spirit users considered their own brand to be "safer" than other cigarettes. This false belief was based only on a word "natural" and a picture of Native American.

You need to spend some time to review your local labeling rules so you can get what you expect. Unfortunately until USDA and other agencies catch up to manufacturers that is the only way. Right now you can find such claims as "farm fresh" that are meaningless and are not regulated in any way. You need to keep an eye for such deceit.

Unscrupulous manufacturers are even manufacturing organic vodka. As if being "organic" makes it better in any way.

Alcohol is the third product you need avoid. Eliminate alcohol from your life completely just like processed foods.

You may be using alcohol to relax or even in order to help you fall asleep as it has a sedative effect. You may be thinking that a glass of wine to unwind at the end of the day is fine. Unfortunately your attempts at self-medication have an opposite effect as initial calming effect is short-lived but the negative impact on your anxiety lasts long after consumption of a beverage.

Ill effects of alcohol will be felt within just a few hours after consumption. Anxiety and Depression Association of America does not leave any room for interpretation. Studies have shown that even a small amount of alcohol increases anxiety, irritability, or depression just a few hours after consumption.

If you feel that you may need assistance join support group or ask people close to you for help. In order to move forward you need to deal with this dependency.

You drink because you have anxiety. Your anxiety increases in severity due to your drinking. This is a chain that needs to be broken. I told you from the beginning that you will have to take steps that will require willpower but the reward waiting for you is worth it.

Use techniques we discussed in previous chapter to deal with withdrawal symptoms and keep your eyes on the prize.

What you stand to gain is happiness, calm, improved health, clear mind and confidence. On the other hand we have products you are giving up. These are products that have been poisoning you for years.

Make the right decision and make a commitment right now.

3.2. WHAT TO USE

Products you consume can increase or decrease your anxiety. Avoiding excessive intake of caffeine as well as cutting processed foods and alcohol from your life will have a powerful effect on the state of your health. Further improvements will be achieved by adopting healthier eating and drinking habits.

Diet plays an important role in anxiety management. Follow healthy guidelines such as eating a balanced diet, drinking enough of water to stay hydrated and stick to complex carbohydrates. You need to consider what you drink, what and when you eat.

Your goal is to maintain a more even blood sugar level, increase antioxidant intake and to ensure sufficient amount of necessary minerals and vitamins.

This might sound overwhelming but in fact it is not. It involves following recommended product list and sticking to a routine you will build around healthier products and habits.

Person can survive without food for weeks but it takes only few days to perish without water. Over half of your body mass is water so it is sufficiently evident that hydration is an extremely important component to correct function of your body and as a result it has a significant influence on your anxiety level.

The key here is to drink water often and in small amounts. Tea, coffee and especially sugary drinks do not count. Sugary drinks and adding sugar to coffee or tea should be avoided. Food already has enough of it.

You may be wondering how is it possible to keep track of your water intake. You can find various recommendations for specific amounts you need to drink in one day. They are highly inaccurate as you need to take into consideration your weight, how much and what you eat and all other variables.

Have some water handy at all times and drink it in regular intervals. Only rule you need to keep in mind - if you feel thirsty you are dehydrated. When you are working keep a glass of water on your desk. When you go out bring a small bottle of water with you.

Listen and feel your body. It will give you feedback if you had enough and in a few days you will find the right rhythm.

"Carbs" have been getting a lot of bad press lately but this negative attention is undeserved. Carbohydrates are an energy source in food that comes from starch, sugar and cellulose. Carbohydrates provide vitamins, minerals, antioxidants and fiber in the diet.

Problem is oversimplification. Carbs get bad press because current health crisis is due to the high intake of simple carbohydrates. Processed foods are full of simple carbohydrates and other ingredients that have negative effect on your health and anxiety.

You can find healthy carbohydrates in foods like vegetables, wheat, rice, corn, oats, barley, quinoa, sorghum, spelt, rye and in fruits, and legumes.

For your convenience I compiled a list of foods that reduce your anxiety:

- Leafy greens (for example, spinach), Swiss card, legumes, nuts, seeds and whole grains. These products are rich in magnesium. Magnesium is required for the proper functioning of nerves, muscles, and many other parts of the body.

- Beef, egg yolks, cashews, liver and oysters. These products are rich in zinc. Enzymes containing zinc are necessary for the synthesis of serotonin. Serotonin is thought to be especially active in constricting smooth muscles, transmitting impulses between nerve cells, regulating cyclic body processes and contributing to well-being and happiness.

- Fatty fish (for instance, salmon) and other products rich in omega-3 fatty acid. Omega-3 affects functionality of the neurotransmitter serotonin, which plays a critical role in both depression and anxiety.

- Fermented milk products (for example, yogurt, kefir), pickles, sauerkraut and other pro-biotic rich foods. Studies have shown that patients who received food rich in pro-biotics had significantly decreased levels of anxiety and depression. In addition, they had significant decreases in systemic inflammation, significantly lower insulin levels, reduced insulin resistance, and a significant rise in glutathione, the body's master antioxidant.

- Asparagus. Depression and anxiety have been linked to folic acid deficiency in the body, and asparagus is one of the top food sources of this nutrient.

- Avocado, almonds. These products contain necessary B vitamins and are high in monounsaturated fats, which help stabilize blood sugar spikes that can cause fatigue, headaches, and trouble concentrating.

Food high in antioxidants:

- Vegetables: spinach, broccoli, kale, artichoke, beets.

- Fruits: plums, cherries, prunes, apples.

- Beans.

- Berries: strawberry, cranberry, raspberry, blueberry, blackberry.

- Nuts.

It is important to remember that you should stay away from processed products. Even if ready-to-eat meal boasts a number of these ingredients this will not make it any better. During processing ingredients are stripped of their nutrients, minerals and vitamins.

Go for fresh, dried, canned or frozen ingredients. Ingredients do not have to be consumed right away and fresh. Canning, drying and freezing processes do not eliminate nutritional properties of the ingredients.

This allows you to make food preparation extremely convenient. Simply buy fresh ingredients on your day off, use them to prepare meals for workweek, freeze them and during the week simply cook by putting ready meal into the oven. Healthy food can be fast.

Healthy food can be fast but I recommend not to strive only for convenience. Cooking can be fun and relaxing. Enjoy experimenting with ingredients and this can become your favorite hobby or even your new career.

Improving your diet with complex carbohydrates will smooth out your blood sugar level and eliminate spikes and drops that manifested in inflated levels of anxiety.

Supplements are another way to get vitamins and minerals but they are unnecessary as a well balanced diet will ensure that you get all the necessary elements to keep you healthy. Supplements are mostly unregulated and due to that it is almost impossible to say if what is indicated on the bottle is what you are actually getting. FDA moves in only if the use of certain product results in poisoning.

Unfortunately supplements send thousands of people to emergency room each year.

This is your choice but due to both of those reasons I can not recommend you to take supplements.

Products indicated above will provide you with all the minerals and vitamins you need to reduce your anxiety, keep you healthy and ready to face any challenge. Adopt healthy eating habits and you will experience radical positive changes in the way you feel mentally and physically.

CHAPTER 4

HABITS

We are creatures of habit. Having a routine allows us to go through the day. Another option would be to think everything through and that would be a slow and exhausting process. Imagine if you had to think about everything you are going to do like, for instance, waking up and taking a moment to think which leg first you should step from the bed.

Habits are helpful but if we build bad habits they keep us in a downward spiral.

You will have to step outside your comfort zone and change your habits that have been ruining your health and had a negative effect on your mental state. Adopting positive habits feels somewhat uncomfortable at first. This is completely natural. Your current habits took time to form so adopting new ones will take some time to stick as well.

4.1. EATING AND DRINKING HEALTHY

First habit you need to adopt is a healthy diet. Keep yourself hydrated by having a source of water handy at all times. Eating healthy is a hard habit to adopt but luckily we live in an age of Internet and it is full of great tasting healthy recipes which take up to half an hour to prepare.

You have plenty of responsibilities that demand a lot of energy and leave you very little time. Cooking meals can be a great way to unwind and preparing portions for two meals makes overall time spent on food preparation less than unfreezing and cooking out-of-the box food.

You can find instructions on what you should eat and drink in the previous chapter.

4.2. SMILING

Thich Nhat Hanh said about a smile *"Because of your smile, you make life more beautiful."* Smile as often as you can. Start your day by smiling into a mirror, smile while you brush your teeth. Tell yourself that this will be a great day. Do this even if you do not feel like it and it feels silly.

Our facial expressions depend on how we feel but it actually works other way around. Studies have shown that smiling releases serotonin - a neurotransmitter that produces feelings of happiness and well-being. It is like a circle of happiness. Smile and you feel happy, you feel happy and you smile.

You can alter the way you feel by putting on a big smile. This might feel a little bit silly but little bit of silliness is a good thing. Sometimes we get so preoccupied with tasks and issues that we loose all joy of life. Little bit of silliness will help you bring back some of the joy of life you used to have.

Sometimes we need a little bit of help to get us started. Try to visualize a happy memory or a funny moment from your favorite comedy. I love slapstick comedies so every time I have difficulty putting on a smile I remember funny moment from the Police Squad! or any other silly Leslie Nielsen movie.

Smiling will bring many advantages to your life as this habit will change how you feel and how people perceive you. Mother Teresa noted the importance of a smile,*"Let us always meet each other with smile, for the smile is the beginning of love."*

Smiling makes you look more approachable, friendly, warm and sincere. Building relationships requires both parties to be ready to open up and to allow another person to share worries, joys and experiences. Smile is an invitation.

Adopting the habit of smiling will allow your current relationships to improve and to build new ones. A simple smile is a very important tool you have to use to improve how you feel and to improve your life.

4.3. SLEEPING

Sleep is a mystery. We know that it is vital to get enough of sleep but scientists still can not pin point the reason why. Good sleep routine is vital for the physical and mental health. English dramatist Thomas Dekker expressed the importance of smiling very precisely, *"Sleep is the golden chain that ties health and our bodies."*

We are all aware of the risks involved in drunk driving but some countries are expanding a list of risks that they are taking into account. Studies have proven beyond any reasonable doubt that drowsiness is as dangerous as being drunk. Sleepiness affects your ability to concentrate, slows your reaction time, affects your ability to process information and impairs your memory. Truck drivers are already legally required to stop and have a rest and with risks involved it is no wonder that police officers are now checking regular drivers for drowsiness as well.

Sleep or lack of it affects your health as it is essential to get enough of quality rest in order to have a strong immune system. Study after study has revealed that people who sleep poorly are at a greater risk of getting sick or developing other health issues. Lack of sleep is one of the factors negatively influencing anxiety levels and your ability to deal with stress.

Long commute, work and other obstacles can make getting enough of sleep a mission impossible. You may feel pressured to get 8 hours of sleep a night but good news is that this rule does not necessarily apply to you. The number of hours you need depends on many factors and you should not feel pressured to get those 8 hours. Most adults can get enough of rest with 6 hours of sleep.

You can implement few changes that will help you fall asleep faster and improve the quality of your sleep.

These few simple improvements to your daily routine will help you get the rest you need:

- Do not use any electronic devices at least 1 hour before going to bed. It is important to prime your body for sleep. Do not watch TV or use any mobile device at least an hour before going to bed. This includes ebook readers. Spend this hour prepping your body for sleep by reading a book while sipping a cup of herbal tea and working on this program.

- No food at least 2 hours before sleeping. Plan your day in such a way that the last meal of the day is not too late.

- Evening is time to get ready for sleep so avoid caffeine. Skip coffee or black tea during the dinner and drink water or fruit tea instead. Avoid juice as it has high sugar content. By drinking beverages containing caffeine you are making it harder for yourself to fall asleep and once you are asleep, caffeine tends to cause nightmares.

- Eliminate light sources from your bedroom. Make your bedroom as dark as you can during the night. Due to a large number of various devices modern home contain, your bedroom might look like Star Trek control panel at night. Cover all those flashing lights as well.

- Go to sleep at a consistent time. Always be in bed at the same time. Your body will go into a pattern and falling asleep will be automatic. You might be inclined to stay up late on weekends to catch up to the show you missed during the work week but you need to go to sleep and to wake up at the same time during the weekend as well.

- Exercise. Increased physical activity improves your mood, health and reduces your risk of developing insomnia.

- Spend five minutes right before going to sleep writing down your plan for tomorrow. Recent studies have shown that writing a to-do list will 'offload' thoughts about tasks that need to be done and this reduces worry and allows you to fall asleep faster.

You may be inclined to cut corners and use alcohol or sleeping pills. Damage alcohol causes to your anxiety is extensively covered in the previous chapter. To give you a quick recap, alcohol has a direct negative effect on your organs and your nervous system. Any short term relief you might feel at the time of the alcohol intake is short lived as it is quickly replaced by spike in anxiety.

Drinking alcohol to get good nights rest is like smoking few cigarettes to improve your performance during a marathon. Alcohol blocks REM sleep and affects normal production of chemicals in your body. You end up waking up without actually getting the necessary rest. You may think that you need to sleep longer but the real solution is the elimination of alcohol and the same amount or even less time of sleep will allow you to get the rest you were dreaming about for so long.

Imagine waking up full of energy and well rested. This reason alone is enough to quit drinking.

The use of sleeping pills is a sensitive subject and you may be using them right now. Mounting evidence suggests that sleeping pills are as damaging to your health as smoking a pack of cigarettes a day.

Sleeping pills are thought to cause drowsiness, delayed reaction times and impaired balance, which can lead users to fall and break their bones. Research has shown that the risk of a fracture is doubled in those who rely on the drugs to get a good night's sleep. A study published online in June 2015 by the American Journal of Public Health found that people prescribed sleeping pills were around twice as likely to be in car crashes as other people.

List of possible side effects is long and worrisome. Long term studies show that sleeping pills can increase heart attack risk by a whopping 50%. Nottingham University researchers found that common pills may also increase the risk of contracting pneumonia and dying from it.

You may be risking your health to gain very limited benefits. Review of one of the leading over-the-counter brand of sleeping aid effectiveness has revealed that people who took a sleeping pill every night for three months fell asleep just 6 minutes faster on average than those who took a placebo. And those who used sleeping aid slept on average only 16 minutes longer than people given a placebo.

If you rely on sleeping pills right now be aware of the risks involved. Employ tactics we discussed above and hopefully soon you will be able to sleep without the chemical assistance. Used on a short-term basis, with the guidance of a physician, sleeping aids can help to break the difficult and often intractable cycle of insomnia and help get sleep back on track. However, the best long-term strategy is to develop a strong, sustainable sleep routine that does not rely on prescription sleep medication. There is no question this takes work, but the rewards are worth it. Your sleep, your overall health will be better for it.

4.4. EXERCISE

Development of anxiety disorders is closely connected to low levels of physical activity. It is extremely luring to fall into a daily routine. You wake up, go to work, come back home, watch some TV or play games and go to sleep. You feel exhausted and doing exercises seems like an impossible task.

A huge hurdle is a perceived lack of time. For most of us days are so crammed that the only option is either to do sports or to get some sleep. This is a problem that solves itself but you have to overcome initial resistance. All these habits require you to keep track of your days and to change what you consume, how you spend your days, evenings and nights.

Exercise is a powerful tool to improve your physical and mental health. All of these healthy habits are beneficial but you will feel significant results only if you employ all of them. Healthy habits multiply positive effects of each other.

Healthy eating and sleeping habits boost your energy levels and this gives you additional energy to exercise. Exercising improves your sleep and your health and this in turn allows you to reach for new challenges in your exercising routine and so on. This is the amplifying effect in action.

Exercise does not mean that you have to spend at least 1 hour at the gym each day and get a six-pack. Exercising means increasing your physical activity in your day-to-day life. You may not have possibility to spend time and money on a gym but tweaks to your daily routine will add up to produce amazing results.

Solution to the lack of time for exercise is replacement of current activities. Instead of watching TV, relax by going for a walk or a run. During your lunch brake you can go outside and eat your lunch outside. Any time you have left - spend it by walking few times around the block.

This simple change in your routine will work wonders. You will return to work refreshed and full of energy to finish tasks instead of just coasting for the rest of the day. Sometimes we get caught up thinking about obstacles and fail to notice solutions that are right in front of us.

Making this change has greatly improved my life and I implore you to do it. I used to eat my lunch either at my desk or in our break-room. I was able to tackle tasks for the first half of the day but after lunch I would feel as if my head was an empty box. Spending some time outside and that small exercise is like pressing a restart button.

It is as important to rest as it is to work. Exercising and being outside allows you to get necessary rest from your work and allows you to tackle tasks much more efficiently. This will reduce stress and overwork as your tasks will be finished on time and you will not have to fix mistakes.

Working while you are tired can be worse than doing nothing. You are much more prone to making mistakes which require you to review and fix everything again later. This way exercise and rest save you time.

Not getting enough of exercise hurts your immune system by reducing your ability to fight infections. Exercise causes changes in antibodies and white blood cells (WBC). WBCs are the body's immune system cells that fight disease. These antibodies or WBCs circulate more rapidly, so they could detect illnesses earlier than they might have before.

Finally, exercise slows down the release of stress hormones. Stress increases your chance of becoming ill and it has direct influence on your anxiety level. In his biography Arnold Schwarzenegger expressed this very precisely, *"Training gives us an outlet for suppressed energies created by stress and thus tones the spirit just as exercise conditions the body."*

You do not need to start lifting weights or running marathons. Being overzealous with exercise can be damaging if you are just starting out. Simply walk everywhere, take the stairs and use any opportunity to be physically active.

The best thing you can do is to join a team. It can be basketball, badminton or any other team sport. Being a member of the team will allow you to get mutual support, spend great time with new friends and it will be harder for you to quit as you will be committed to the team.

4.5. QUIT SMOKING

Smoking is nowhere near as common as it used to be just a few years ago but if you are one of the last ones to rely on cigarette to fight anxiety listen up.

For the sake of your health you have to quit.

Studies have unambiguously debunked myth that smoking reduces anxiety. Research has proven beyond any doubt that the opposite is true. Cigarette companies decided to tackle public health concerns by introducing other products like e-cigarette.

Anything with nicotine in it has a strong negative effect on you. E-cigarettes and similar products have been introduced with slogans that these are safe alternatives to regular cigarettes. Studies take time and now that the results are starting to come in it looks like e-cigarette is safer than regular cigarette but it still poses many long term health risks.

Nicotine by itself is a very nasty thing and you should not rely on it to reduce your anxiety.

Nicotine is a highly addictive chemical which affects nervous system and has a negative effect on your anxiety level. There are three main mechanisms how nicotine affects your mental state.

First, the ritual of smoking may feel like it reduces your stress and anxiety but calming effect is short-lived. Nicotine has a very short half-life. You feel the urge to smoke because you experience withdrawal symptoms. This makes you feel additional anxiety multiple times a day and this adds to your overall level of anxiety and stress. You are trying to fight fire by pouring gasoline on it.

Second reason is a failure to cope with anxiety on your own. Smoking essentially replaces your own natural ability to cope. Stress coping is a mental skill, when you do not use it, you lose it. Smoking temporarily numbs anxiety but it does not actually help you cope, so your ability to cope with stress without the use of nicotine deteriorates.

This is the main reason most smokers fail to quit. Relying on smoking to cope with stress means that you loose your ability to deal with even a minor amount of stress without it. Smoking restrictions are constantly being expanded so an ability to cope with anxiety without the assistance of nicotine is essential skill you need to posses.

Finally, smoking exposes you to a huge number of dangerous chemicals. Healthy lifestyle is simply incompatible with smoking as cigarette smoke contains huge variety of cancerogens, poison and trash. Smoking or using other nicotine sources feeds addiction that ruins your health.

Smoking has the same effect on your body as experiencing stress. Your heart rate increases, your blood pressure shoots up and this closely resembles effects of stress. Your body feels these symptoms and it reacts accordingly.

Negative effects of smoking are well documented and are readily available to you in a huge number of reputable sources. You made excuses in the past but now you made a commitment.

If you want to eliminate panic attacks from your life and reduce anxiety to normal levels you have to quit smoking. There is no place for half-measures as all these changes will have significant effect only if you employ all of them.

CHAPTER 5

SETTING GOALS

Anxiety management tactics we covered so far are great in a short and middle term. Continuous dedication and adoption of these tactics into your daily routine will eliminate panic attacks and reduce your anxiety but getting your anxiety under control permanently requires further work. Long term anxiety management requires analysis, review and alteration of how you perceive the world around you.

Anxiety management is an ongoing process that requires diligence and determination. To keep your eyes on the prize you will set goals you want to achieve. Setting goals is a great exercise as it diverts your efforts and gives your endeavors purpose.

Without a specific, articulated purpose you can spend a lot of time and waste a lot of effort without any significant result. Water can fall on the ground harmlessly or it can break any barrier. If you are not focused on your effort, your effort will bear no fruit like water falling harmlessly during the rain. It takes concentrated effort and determination to achieve your goals.

Your actions require a clear purpose which is specific enough. It is not enough to tell yourself that you want to be happy. What happiness means to you?

We all have limited resources and one resource which we have to take into account the most is time. Time is the reason why you can not afford to have vague goals in your life because you will only end up always lagging behind, trying to catch up to a number of goals which are slipping away.

This is a great source of anxiety on its own. Setting clear priorities will eliminate conflicts that you have to deal with on a daily basis. You will have guidelines for your life you can use to make quick and clear decisions.

My priorities in life, in order of their significance, are family, health and my career. Having clear priorities removes anxiety that stems from indecision or second-guessing.

Setting goals has another great effect - having clear goals gives you additional strength. People were able to overcome insurmountable obstacles to achieve their goals. Goals you feel passionate about will give you powerful motivation and a feeling that you can achieve anything.

Keep these goals always in your sight. You can put them on your fridge or on your bathroom mirror so it is the first thing you see every day. Share your goals with people closest to you. They will provide you with support and help you achieve your goals.

Take a moment to think about what are your main priorities in life. Write them down in an order of their importance. Do not set more than five priorities as not to dilute your attention.

MY MAIN PRIORITIES

1.

2.

3.

4.

5.

Now that you have your priorities straight you can make plans and set goals. Write down a short story about your typical day after you end this program without fear and worry controlling your life. Give this story tangibility by adding details. Create a short movie with your words about your day starting with you waking up and ending with you falling asleep happy and without any difficulty.

Focus on events as they happen and your feelings now that you are not under the thumb of anxiety. Be sure to include your new healthy habits.

Review your story and note events and feelings. For example, you might have written that you had to do a presentation in front of an important client and you felt calm, confident and persuasive. Details in your story uncover your desires. Use these to help you write up to five goals you set yourself for the next two weeks.

TWO WEEK GOALS

1.

2.

3.

4.

5.

Write down goals you set for yourself for half a year. Two week goals have to be as specific as you can make them. Your goals for the middle term can be less specific but avoid being too vague.

SIX MONTH GOALS

1.

2.

3.

4.

5.

Finally you need to set yourself long term goals. These goals reflect your main values and priorities.

LONG TERM GOALS

1.

2.

3.

Goals, even long term, are not meant to remain constant. Review and update your goals constantly to keep them relevant. This is especially true for short term goals.

Use these goals to give you drive to grow and improve yourself and to achieve happiness you deserve. Earl Nightingale stressed the importance of having clear goals, *"People with goals succeed because they know where they are going."*

CHAPTER 6

PERCEPTION FALLACIES

Nobody is born with allergies. Allergens, or molecules with the potential to cause allergy, are everywhere in our environment. They come in the form of tree pollen, food, mold, dust mites, snake or insect venom, and animals, such as cats, dogs, and cockroaches. When the body mistakes one of these substances as a threat and reacts with an immune response, we develop an allergy.

Anxiety is a part of a mechanism designed to keep you safe and alive which is called "fight or flight" response. The process of anxiety disorder development is very similar to the development of allergies, as these are both dysfunctional reactions of a protective mechanism which adjusts itself to work in a highly sensitive setting.

Modern life is filled with various stimuli. Compared to fighting a pack of wolves, modern life should seem like a vacation but the stream of decisions and challenges you face is constant and much more rapid compared to what this system was originally designed to handle. No wonder mechanism went haywire especially bearing in mind that, as an option, *flight* part has almost entirely been eliminated.

Anxiety disorders have their roots in real life in the form of challenges you face and in this sense anxiety is objective but the level of your anxiety is completely subjective. The only thing which determines the severity of your anxiety is the way you interpret information you receive.

Anxiety stems from the faulty ways of thinking that convince us of a reality that is simply not true. Recognizing these faulty ways is the first step in the process of a long term anxiety management.

Note reality distortions you are using, as recognition of these distortions allows you to stop this mechanism. Currently these distortions work automatically. Anxiety management requires you to actively take over and reprogram the way you interpret events.

6.1. FILTERING

Over 16 000 flights are in the air at any given moment and all of them will land safely with an extremely rare exception. Flying is the safest form of travel but fear of flying is one of the most common phobias.

Most of the blame for this lies with the coverage of flying. We do not hear about millions of flights that ended successfully. We hear about flying on the news only when there is either a delayed flight horror story or a crash. We get only bad news and this forms a very negative image of a situation.

This is called filtering. Filtering is distortion of reality wherein you focus only on the negative and completely ignore the positive. Even if you have an abundance of positive and goods things happening, you focus on negative even if it is a small aspect.

Filtering blocks you from seeing positive as well as not allowing you to enjoy good fortune or your achievements.

6.2. CATASTROPHIZING

You may have seen doomsday movies *2012* or *San Andreas*. They took real possible event of an earthquake in San Andreas Fault and expanded on what might happen to such an extent that these movies became parodies with nothing in common with science or even common sense. These movies might seem ridiculous but you may be doing the same thing to yourself if you are catastrophizing.

This distortion makes you overemphasize any negative event and in hand with over-thinking you end up certain that the worst possible outcome is bound to happen. Even the smallest mistake can trigger this response. For instance, you may make a mistake in a memo. You start to think that the worst thing is sure to happen and you convince yourself that this is the only possible turn of events. You imagine that your boss notices this mistake and based on this insignificant mistake decides to fire you.

Same way this distortion does not allow you to be happy about your achievements as you end up convincing yourself of their insignificance.

It is uncommon for people to think that this way they are "preparing" themselves for a negative outcome and this way it will not feel that bad once it occurs. You may be using this reasoning but it is completely wrong. Wasting time and energy on thinking about what wrong may happen does not prepare you for anything. This activity results only in negative outlook on the world, stress and anxiety.

6.3. BLACK AND WHITE THINKING

Life is all about nuances but this distortion limits you only to all-or-nothing thinking. This perception fallacy makes you think that you must be perfect at every endeavour you undertake or you are a failure. You may think that it is good to hold yourself to a higher standard but you end up putting too much pressure on yourself.

We are humans and it is impossible for us to be good at everything and be able to catch every little detail. Henry Ford did not attribute his success to himself alone. He knew that it is impossible for one person to know everything about production processes, management, marketing and thousands of other areas, which require specialized experience. He said, "*I am not the smartest, but I surround myself with smartest people.*" He knew that it is impossible to be an expert in everything.

Mr. Ford made mistakes and some of them were spectacular in their magnitude. Biggest mistakes are done when successful people start believing that their success is solely due to their brilliance and become deaf to advice of people they relied on to make them a success.

Black and white thinking is an expectation that objectively can not be achieved. It is impossible to be great and infallible at everything as well as being bad at one thing does not make you a failure. Making a mistake simply means that you are bad at one thing and good at another.

6.4. JUMPING TO CONCLUSIONS

Jumping to conclusions is one of the most common forms of negative thinking. Jumping to conclusions refers to a tendency to be sure of something without any evidence at all.

Jumping to conclusions is like owning a crystal ball that predicts only misery.

This is not a new tendency. Epictetus, who lived in the first century, wrote *"As you think, so you become… Our busy minds are forever jumping to conclusions, manufacturing and interpreting signs that are not there."*

It is natural for us to make assumptions and inferences about whatever is occurring in our environment. Jumping to conclusions is a natural way for us to interpret events as it allows us to react to events faster. This becomes hindrance if your assumptions are almost exclusively negative and are only slightly based on available information or have nothing in common with reality at all.

For example, your partner may ask you to have lunch with him/her and you assume that he/she is going to break up with you. You arrive pale as a piece of paper to find out that your partner simply was hungry and wanted to have lunch with you.

6.5. OVERGENERALI-ZATION

Overgeneralization is an error that involves coming to a conclusion based on information that is too general and/or not specific enough. This fallacy is similar to jumping to conclusions, the only difference between these two fallacies is that when you overgeneralize, your negative assumptions are based on real event, which acts as a trigger.

The most dangerous conclusions we develop by overgeneralizing are limiting beliefs. If you are prone to this fallacy you create negative beliefs about yourself and the world around you, which can be based on a single experience.

For instance, you may try to talk to someone you are attracted to and it goes badly. You overgeneralize and based on this single interaction you make a decision that you are bad at talking to men/women.

Time goes by and you forget the original event. You are left with a negative belief that stops you from even trying to approach people you feel attracted to. We are all born with similar capabilities. People you admire and envy, who seem to be better at everything you do, are not born this way. They worked long and hard, they encountered and overcame multiple setbacks before they gained enough experience to be able to do what they do with apparent ease. This applies to everything from speaking to a person you like to being in charge of multinational corporation.

Making a mistake is simply the part of a learning process.

6.6. MISLABELING

This is an extreme form of overgeneralization in which you make extreme negative assumptions about yourself or the world around you based on a single event. One single bad experience is enough to destroy your self belief or completely ruin how you view the world around you.

Imagine that you are on a holiday and on the first day after you exit souvenir shop you notice that you were given wrong change. Based on this single event mislabeling distortion makes you assume that everyone in this state or country is a thieving scumbag. In reality, cashier made an honest mistake.

Similarly, mislabeling ruins how you view yourself, as all it takes is a single mistake for you to conclude that you are bad at everything.

This faulty thinking has a tendency of radicalizing your attitude towards everything and it makes you describe events in a language which is highly emotionally loaded. For example, light turns green but the driver in front of you fails to start going right away so you mutter under your breath, "Stupid idiot. Learn to drive before going on a road."

You will be hard pressed to find anyone who has not said similar things to blow off some steam but it becomes a problem if you find yourself doing this constantly.

6.7. ALWAYS BEING RIGHT

Belief that you are always right is another fallacy that puts you on the spot and makes you hold yourself to a ridiculously high standard. I consider myself a well read person. I like to relax by watching documentaries or reading educational magazines but I know that there are large gaps in my knowledge.

It is impossible to be always right. You may consider this distortion as your advantage. Holding yourself to a higher standard is a good thing but to consider that you are always right means that you are deaf to arguments and reason.

This distortion puts a lot of strain on your relationships and on the ability of others to work with you. Trying to get your point across to a person with a belief that she/he is infallible is like trying to communicate with a brick wall as all arguments fall on a deaf ear. Another person is left feeling frustrated and humiliated as such demeanor clearly indicated that her or his opinion is not valued.

Finally, when you inevitably encounter a situation, when you are faced with the undeniable fact that you are wrong, your self image and your confidence implode.

Accepting that you can be wrong is not a sign of weakness but a sign of strength. Only a confident person is comfortable enough with herself/himself to listen and accept other points of view.

6.8. BLAMING

John Burroughs said, "A person can fail many times, but he/she is not a failure until he/she begins to blame somebody else."

Blaming can be justified if misfortune we experience is a result of someone else acting in a wrong way or negative outcome was caused by objective circumstances. For instance, you would be completely right to blame another driver if you there hit even though you had the right of way.

Blaming becomes a fallacy of perception when we start attributing blame to others for the way we feel or the way we act. If you have this distortion you end up spending energy by looking for someone to blame instead of working on yourself.

Robert Anthony noticed this risk, *"When you blame others, you give up your power to change."*

You can not control what other people do. You are responsible only for your actions and your emotions.

6.9. PERSONALIZATION

Personalization distortion makes you believe that everything you do has a direct impact on external events or other people, no matter how far-fetched the link may be. This distortion makes you feel like bad things are happening all around you and no matter what you do, you had a direct hand in the negative outcome of those events.

For example, you may hear that someone was let go at work and you immediately assign blame for this to yourself because some time ago you made a comment to a co-worker about this person. Reasons can be extremely trivial and link may be completely irrational.

This fallacy of perception stops you from doing anything as you feel as if no matter what you do other people end up suffering. You assign yourself an unreasonably important role and view yourself as a cause of nearly every event happening around you.

6.10. CONTROL FALLACY

During an interview rally driver was asked if he had any superstitions. He answered that he used to wear one shirt which he never washed but he crashed once, twice and finally from then on he races wearing clean shirts.

Superstition is a form of control fallacy as it allows us to feel as if certain actions or use of "lucky" things will have an impact on external events we can not have any control over.

Control fallacy can manifest itself in a belief either that everything happening is influenced by you or you may think that nothing depends on you. Both beliefs are equally wrong as the truth is in the middle.

Our actions have an impact on certain events but a lot of things happening are determined by external factors. Your dedication and diligence in following advice presented in this book will have a direct impact on your anxiety, allowing you to feel happy and full of energy. On the other hand, no matter how much you will knock on wood it will not have any impact on future events.

6.11. EMOTIONAL REASONING

Richard H. Thaler received Nobel prize in 2017 for his contributions to behavioural economics. His contribution was the expansion of economic models with a simple truth - people are irrational. We are emotional beings and emotional reasoning fallacy takes this to the next level.

This distortion removes any objectivity from our reasoning. You abandon any external proof and base your beliefs only on how you feel. Abandonment of external verification makes your state extremely unstable as it is a subject to sudden changes.

You can feel great about yourself but only one unsuccessful interaction or negative comment you heard can change that. For instance, if you feel boring and unattractive you do not question these feelings and simply accept that you are boring and unattractive. There may be plenty of evidence to suggest the opposite but you do not question your feelings.

6.12. FALLACY OF FAIRNESS

Life is not a Disney cartoon and due to that sometimes it can be unfair. We all have a sense of fairness but if you have this distortion you are taking this to extreme.

We are taught by our parents, school, church and media that our actions will be rewarded or we will receive punishment. You may have grown up with a sense that if you do everything right you should receive rewards.

Strong feeling of fairness can result in a bitter disappointment and resentment.

Life is a complicated series of events. People who deserve punishment sometimes get away scot-free. Look at the banking crisis of 2008. Most of the people responsible for bringing so much misery to so many people got away on their golden parachutes.

Similarly, it is not given that your actions will receive reward you may feel you deserve.

6.13. FALLACY OF CHANGE

The fallacy of change lies in an expectation that other people will change as it suits you. You can control how you feel and how you act but nobody is obliged to change.

For example, you may be dissatisfied with your boss and feel under-appreciated. You need your boss to change in order for you to be happy.

This distortion makes you believe that someone else needs to change for you to be happy. This attitude is unproductive as it removes you as a factor from ensuring your own happiness. The fallacy of change removes you from the driving seat and makes you a passenger in your own life.

6.14. SHOULDS

"Shoulds" refers to living in accordance to arbitrary rules. You create expectations for how you and everyone else is supposed to act in all situations. Expectation that everyone else is going to follow these rules is bound to be shattered.

Other people can not be upheld responsible for breaking rules they are not even aware exist.

For instance, you may have an expectation that waiter should ask you how you are doing when they approach the table for the first time. Busy waiter comes by and politely takes your order but never asks how was your day. She/he broke your unwritten rule so you got angry and the whole nice evening you had planned was ruined.

Similarly, putting down arbitrary rules for yourself creates unnecessary inner conflict which is a source of anxiety and disappointment.

6.15. HEAVEN'S REWARD FALLACY

The heaven's reward fallacy is an expectation that any sacrifice or self-denial you make will be rewarded. This distortion is similar to the fallacy of fairness and is based on a similar belief that world is like a game wherein you accrue points. In popular culture this is manifested in a belief in "karma."

This fallacy can result in a very long and grueling suffering while you wait for your reward to come. Denying yourself happiness does not ensure good fortune in the future.

Similarly, if you expect that taking on additional responsibilities and tasks will result in praise or reward, you are priming yourself for a disappointment. Your primary motivator should be your satisfaction in achieving goals, self realization, etc. Removal of unsubstantiated expectation of reward and switching your motivation back to you will remove anxiety this fallacy causes.

For example, you may be going to the gym. Your primary motivator is a desire to hear compliments from your partner. Naturally you get discouraged when those compliments are not said and you are angry at your partner while she/he is left dumbfounded what did he/she do wrong.

These 15 fallacies are responsible for your anxiety and in the next chapter you will find seven techniques to address or reverse these distortions. Before you move on to the next chapter check if you noted fallacies you feel are the most applicable to you. You may find it hard to select up to 5 as all of us are plagues by all of these fallacies at some point.

Do not search for the single most suitable fallacy as it is common to have multiple reality perception fallacies. Note 3 - 5 distortions you feel are the most applicable to you.

My perception fallacies:

1. _____

2. _____

3. _____

4. _____

5. _____

CHAPTER 7

7 STEPS TO ELIMINATE ANXIETY

There are many techniques and tools used to address anxiety issues. In this chapter you will learn seven techniques that have been shown to be highly effective in decreasing anxiety levels. These techniques work together with lifestyle changes covered in previous chapters.

It takes only a week for significant changes in your anxiety level to be felt due to adjustments you made to your diet and your daily routine. These changes allowed you to significantly reduce your anxiety level and eliminate panic attacks. These next seven steps will ensure long term elimination of anxiety as a limiting factor in your life.

You owe it to yourself to rediscover your old cool, calm and collected self.

You only live once so it only makes sense to enjoy it.

7.1. JOURNALING

Journaling is a technique that allows you to capture events, emotions and thoughts you had during the day and to review them in a safe environment without the distortion of memory. It is similar to keeping a diary but instead of writing down what happened you will write down things as they happen.

Studies have shown that journaling has a positive impact on both physical and mental health. This exercise allows you to become more attuned to your thoughts and to gain skills at turning them around, when they become counterproductive or destructive. Journal is a tool to catch these thoughts, reflect on them and experiment with how a different way of thinking can impact a certain situation.

The main two purposes of the journal is to capture the moment and to learn from it.

Journal is your daily tool you should fill in throughout the day. You need to capture both positive and negative experiences. Your days are filled with activity which eliminated any possibility to stop and reflect as events unfold. Entrusting this task to memory allows for distortions by imagination or you can simply forget what happened.

Later on, after the day has gone by, you can reflect on how you reacted to events of the day and how you felt throughout the day. This will provide very useful insight into how you see yourself and the world around you.

Journal provides a safe environment for not only looking at "what happened" during the day, but to examine how changing your thoughts or behaviors may have brought about a different outcome. Once you have recounted the day's events, you can also spend few minutes journaling about the lessons of the day, and practice alternative ways to react to stress, handle relationships and recognize and appreciate life's positive moments.

Journaling will require your commitment. Write down your experiences throughout the day and commit specific time slot in your day for journaling. Find quiet time and place to journal. For example, many people set aside few minutes at the end of the day or before going to sleep.

SITUATION DETAILS:

What happened?

Where?

When?

Who with?

How?

EMOTIONS / MOODS:

What emotion did I feel at that time? What else? On a scale of 0 -10 how intense emotion did I feel?

PHYSICAL SENSATIONS

What did I notice in my body? Where did I feel it?

UNHELPFUL THOUGHTS OR IMAGES

What went through my mind?

What was it about the situation that disturbed or upset me?

What did those thoughts/images/memories mean to me, or tell me about the situation?

This information is essential for identifying your thought patterns and emotional tendencies, describing them, and finding out how to change, adapt, or cope with them.

7.2. IDENTIFYING FALLACIES

Journal has to become your best friend and confidant. Breathing and muscle relaxation exercises together with lifestyles changes you learned in previous chapters should have already significantly improved the state of your anxiety. This is important because now we will work on recognizing the distortions you are susceptible to and your thought patterns.

Collect data about your daily activities and when you gather information about at least one week, sit down to review this information. We are looking for perception fallacies.

You already know 15 perception fallacies and are aware of at least three fallacies you are most susceptible to use. This will immensely help you to recognize unproductive thought patterns that need to be corrected.

You must become aware of which distortions you are most vulnerable to. Assume everything you think is a perception fallacy until proven otherwise.

This exercise may reveal that distortions you are most commonly using are not the ones you previously identified as your most common fallacies. This is completely normal and actually this is something you should expect.

Continue this exercise and pay close attention to repeating patterns. Similar situations should provoke the use of particular perception distortions. For instance, you may recognize that at work you are prone to Heaven's Reward Fallacy. You are constantly taking on additional tasks and when you do not get immediate praise or rewards, you feel disappointed or even take unconstructive actions like bad-mouthing your boss.

Notice what type of event is the cause of which particular distortion.

We need to grow your awareness of these thought patterns to the point where you are able to recognize them automatically. Reaching this point will allow you to move on to the next step.

I know that you are keen on moving on right away but when you made a commitment, you made a promise to yourself that you will dedicate necessary time and effort. Do not move on to the next step too early.

7.3. THOUGHT RESTRUCTURING

Learning about perception fallacies and noticing them should have been eye opening for you. We have yet to tackle them but you are already aware of how much burden you have been putting on yourself. You are extremely strong because you were able to function even while being weighted down by this load.

Imagine how great your life is going to be without all this weight. It is like training jumping with added weights. Once weights are removed you can jump a distance you previously thought was impossible.

Use your journal to review the use of distorted reality perceptions and change them by using questionnaire you will find below. You need to build your skills so start doing this exercise at the end of the day with a pen and paper.

Later, when you gain enough experience you can apply this technique to stop perception fallacies in the moment.

If you find it difficult to distance yourself from events you experienced, imagine a person you respect. Review situation from the point of view of this person. Imagine what they would think about that thought, what meaning they would give it, and how would they react to it.

Use these Review perception fallacies one by one using these questions:

- Is this thought a fact, or just a thought/opinion?

- What am I reacting to? What meaning am I giving this situation?

- How strong did I feel?

- Is there another way of looking at it?

- What would someone else make of it?

- What advice would I give someone else in this situation?

- Is my reaction in proportion to the actual event?

- How important is this really? How important will it be in a year's time?

- Can I be more flexible in my thinking?

- Which perception fallacy or fallacies did I use? What was the cause of thinking that way?

- What evidence is there that this thought is true?

- What would be a more balanced way of looking at it?

- What positive aspects can I point out?

- What is the bigger picture?

For example, you may have been on a date and you noted that you felt that the person you met was bored. Later you reviewed this event:

Is this thought a fact, or just a thought/opinion?

Answer: Opinion.

Is there another way of looking at it?

Answer: Yes, there is.

What would someone else make of it?

Answer: Someone else would say that it was a nice, relaxing evening. They would recommend me to stop worrying about how the evening goes and simply enjoy it.

What advice would I give someone else in this situation?

Answer: Relax, do not worry so much about what your date is thinking. Enjoy yourself and the person you are with will enjoy himself or herself too. They are most probably nervous as well. Concentrate on yourself and your own happiness. The most important question you need to ask yourself is "did I have a good time?".

Is my reaction in proportion to the actual event?

Answer: No, it was only the second time we met so it is too early to feel any worry about making a bad impression.

How important is this really? How important will it be in a year's time?

Answer: Not at all.

Can I be more flexible in my thinking?

Answer: Yes.

Which perception fallacy or fallacies did I use? What was the cause of thinking that way?

Answer: Shoulds - if people are having a good time there should not be any silent moments; Jumping to Conclusions - he/she thinks I am boring.

What evidence is there that this thought is true?

Answer: None.

What would be a more balanced way of looking at it?

Answer: It is natural that moments of silence occur during a meeting. Both people who participate in a conversation are equally responsible to keep it going. She/he does not find me boring because this was our second date. Even if this was our last date this does not mean that I am boring. This would only mean that we are not suitable for each other.

What positive aspects can I point out?

Answer: I spent an evening in a nice place. I enjoyed listening to this person and enjoyed being listened to. The weather was great. I saw a beautiful bird.

What is the bigger picture?

Answer: This is not a relationship yet so I can concentrate on having a nice time during dates.

Review your journal this way each day. This exercise will build your skills in recognizing perception fallacies and you will learn how to change them. Once you gain enough experience you will be able to do this in real-time.

7.3.1. NOTICE POSITIVES

Daily routine puts us in a habit of concentrating only on the things we have to do, challenges we face, so it is no wonder that we completely loose our ability to stop to appreciate beauty in our lives. Life has a tendency to atrophy our ability to be able to enjoy simple pleasures life has to offer.

Children are able to be happy about anything. They can play for hours with a simple box having time of their lives. You used to be that way as well but somewhere along the way, as you grew up, you lost this sense of wonder.

You feel something similar to that feeling you got in your childhood when you buy yourself nice clothes or a beautiful accessory but it just does not feel the same. Things bring only a short-lived happiness.

Real happiness lies not in more stuff but in your ability to notice and appreciate beauty as well as positive things in your life. We need to reintroduce that sense of wonder you used to have. Henry Ward Beecher is quoted to have said, *"The art of being happy lies in the power of extracting happiness from common things."*

Make a point of noticing positive things in your daily life.

When you are working on thought restructuring, write down as many positive things as you can. Review your day and write as many positive things you encountered that day as you can. Do not let larger events overshadow small details.

These positive things can take any form. It can be someone smiling on the street, beautiful flower or nice way warm wind felt on your skin. Open your eyes and notice these small positive things.

7.4. ON-THE-SPOT THOUGHT RESTRUCTURING

Journaling and thought restructuring will build skills you require to spot perception fallacies and correct them on the spot as they appear. Thought restructuring involves acknowledgement of a thought as a thought, stopping an automatic response and replacing it with a productive reaction.

Our emotions and actions are guided by automatic responses. These automatic responses are learned in a similar way to how habits are formed. You learn to respond to a certain type of event in a particular way. As any habit, this can be altered to better suit your needs and desires.

You are already forming healthy eating and lifestyle habits. In addition to these new habits you have to add new ways to view the world and to respond to it. This entails the use of thought restructuring technique. We need to alter this technique for the "mobile" use in order for it to be effective for on-the- spot employment.

Questionnaire you have above may look cumbersome as it is designed to be applicable for all fallacies and it is designed with the assumption that you are doing this exercise at the end of the day while enjoying a cup of warm tea. With practice you will learn to recognize distortions automatically and to apply the most effective questions which are best suited for particular distortion.

For instance, you may notice an idea is starting to creep in that small mistake you made in the project you are working on will result in a project failure. You recognize that this is catastrophizing fallacy. This requires you to stop for a moment, employ the breathing exercise and as you regain composure ask yourself questions that will allow you to stop the chain of catastrophizing and to put your mind on a productive path. You can ask yourself: "Is this mistake really that big?"; "Can I correct this mistake?", etc.

Below you will find questions that will help you restructure your thoughts and employ productive ways of thinking. You will learn through practice that some questions are more suitable to particular distortions than others. Note and use this to speed up the process.

- What is happening right now? What thoughts, feelings and sensations do I notice?

- Which perception fallacy does this thought corresponds to?

- What am I reacting to? What meaning am I giving this event? How is this affecting me?

- What is the result of my believing this thought?

- What would be the effect of not believing this thought?

- Is this a thought, a feeling, or a sensation?

- How can I defuse from this thought?

- Am I predicting what might happen in the future?

- Am I evaluating a situation? How can I describe it instead?

- Is this a memory from the past?

In addition to asking yourself a question, you may want to write down thought in question, in order to make the process easier, as writing down involves formalization which will ease identification which fallacy this thought, feeling or sensation corresponds to. This is especially beneficial at the beginning of the process so have pen and small notepad handy at all times, or you can use memo app on your phone.

7.5. GOING ALL THE WAY

In order to fight our worries, sometimes we must embrace them.

This exercise will allow you to stop running away from worry and to embrace it. If your main perception fallacy is catastrophizing, this is an especially useful exercise.

The source of abnormal levels of anxiety is not the world around us but our reaction to it and more specifically our fear of worry. You get caught in a vicious cycle of anxiety as it is feeding itself until you are left a shivering husk of your former self.

Creating hypothetical chain of events your action can cause is a very common "past-time" but most probably you never let that chain go all the way. You suppress this chain of events somewhere in the middle by spending a lot of your mental energy or you get overwhelmed.

Thinking what might happen is a very unproductive and damaging activity but for the sake of this exercise you will do this and you will finally bring this chain to the end.

This exercise is very simple and it will allow you to realize two important things:

1. Even if the worst case happens, it is not that bad, and/or

2. This "fortune telling" is ridiculous and makes no sense.

Next time you notice that you have a worry and you are starting to create a chain of events do not suppress it. This time take charge by bringing this chain of hypothetical events to conclusion. It may feel uncomfortable at first but it is completely safe.

I must be honest, I hate it when someone else is driving and I especially hate to be in a passenger seat. This is partly due to me liking to drive but mostly I feel this way because I like to be in control of the car and due to the force of habit it just feels weird to be on the right from my usual position.

Going all the way with the worry chain will allow you to take back control. Instead of trying to fight it, you will actively participate in this activity and this in turn will change how you view worry. Instead of a helpless position now you are in control.

How far you should take this chain? Take it as far as you can get it. Take it to a ridiculous level.

For example, if I lost my pen who can say that this will not result in a nuclear reactor meltdown.

Catastophizing makes no sense so there is no point for you in trying to stay realistic during this exercise. Do this for a few times and you will realize that there is no reason to fear worry. Chain will break as your realization of it's futility will eliminate power your fear gave it in the past.

Oprah Winfrey said, *"The thing you fear most has no power. Your fear of it is what has the power. Facing the truth really will set you free."*

7.6. EXPOSURE

Exposure technique is especially valuable if your anxiety is brought on by specific triggers or if you suffer from obsessive compulsive disorder (OCD). Probably you can guess from the name what this exercise entails.

Simply mentioning that you have to face your trigger most probably brought on your symptoms - your palms may be sweaty, your mouth dried out, heart seems to be beating faster with every second, you feel first drops of sweat appear. This is a completely normal reaction and this is not going to stop you from going forward with this exercise.

You felt this way for a very long time. This fear is triggered automatically so most probably you have not thought about why do you feel this way. It feels like you were born with this obstacle but this obstacle is not something you were predestined to deal with for the rest of your life.

The source of your fear may stem from an experience in your early childhood or source can be something else. This is not something you should worry about as the source is not important. Importance lies only in a way this fear alters your present and in removing this limitation from your life.

I am afraid of heights. I still get mild head-spinning when I look down while I am on a tall building or a hill but in the past similar situation would have left me paralyzed with fear. I just could not walk as my legs became jello.

I faced my fear by jumping with a parachute. Just to be sure - twice.

For a creature that was never meant to fly I consider that my reaction was appropriate but poor instructor, after jumping with me he most probably had to have his ears checked out. It was scary but having a professional to shout instructions at me and training on the ground did not leave much space for fear as I concentrated on what I had to do. Finally, once I was out-there it was so beautiful and humbling that I just could not fear as I was not able to think. I was just trying to take it all in.

This is a drastic example of exposure in action. I did it this way simply because I wanted to get rid of this limitation once and for all. I felt like I was letting my kids down and I brought them pain when they saw me in a state of horror. I wanted to show them that even if you fear something you can step over your fears and achieve anything you put your mind to.

No matter what you fear, this is a learned reaction, not something set in stone. You can change it by exposing yourself to gradually increasing levels of interaction with your feared thing, action or event. Write down your experience and analyze it. Ask someone you trust to help you with this.

If you suffer from an obsessive compulsive disorder, the source of your behavior is expectation of negative consequences if you do not follow set behaviors. In order to address and eliminate this limitation you need to expose yourself to whatever it is that normally elicits compulsive behavior, but do your best to refrain from the compulsive behavior. Combine this with journaling for a greater effectiveness.

It can be very uncomfortable but it will feel this way only for a first few times.

Write down your feelings and write down your expectations of what do you feel this change of behavior might bring. Scale your feelings. You will notice that nothing bad actually happened and with every exposure your anxiety level will gradually drop.

Gradually, fear will loose its grip on you and you will leave it behind allowing you to move towards a brighter future.

7.7. WELCOMING ANXIETY

Louisa May Alcott wrote, *"I am not afraid of storms, for I am learning how to sail my ship."*

Anxiety is not caused by objective realities of the world but stems from your subjective reaction to it. This is your way to interact with the world and due to the subjectivity of this interaction, you can change it. Anxiety makes you feel powerless while in fact you are responsible for your own destiny. You learned to fear anxiety while in fact it is your friend.

Anxiety is simply a mechanism we inherited which controls the fight-or-flight response. This is an essential mechanism for survival of any creature but over-zealous reaction puts you in a state of worry which results in a dreaded anxiety cycle of worrying about worrying.

You learned techniques that allow you to tackle anxiety and your fears. You embraced new habits that tackle anxiety on a physiological level. The final step is inviting anxiety.

Big part of the power anxiety had over you was your resistance to it. That might feel wrong but when it comes to anxiety your resistance only made situation worse. It is like trying to open the door by pushing it. Door will not budge so you try to push it harder but it will not work as you need to pull this door to open it.

You are already doing this as previous exercises guided you in facing your anxiety.

The way you feel is influenced by your actions and vice versa. Your attempts to suppress anxiety were a signal to your brain that this was something that needed to be suppressed. Some pranksters used to perform a prank with public. They would take their friend who was an ordinary person and swarm on him in a public place pretending to be paparazzi. It would not take long before other people would gather and start asking this ordinary person for an autograph and to take a picture with them.

The trigger itself is not important as the way you react to it is the only thing that determines impact of this trigger on you.

Next time you feel onset of fear or anxiety do not try to push it away or fight it. Acknowledge this feeling and welcome it in. Feel how this acceptance has removed power away from anxiety.

The fuel which was fueling your anxiety was your resistance to it. This energy is now diverted towards the positive and is power behind the change this program brings to your life. The amount of energy remains the same but redirection of it allows you to grow as a person, improve your relationships and take opportunities that open up.

Acceptance of anxiety does not mean that you are giving up to it but the opposite. Acceptance of anxiety is changing of the way you interact with anxiety from reaction to action. This action stops you from being a spectator and gives you back the power.

This step is not about stopping anxiety. This whole book is not about stopping anxiety as anxiety is a vital part of your life. What you will achieve is elimination of abnormal reactions to triggers and reduction of your anxiety to normal levels.

In order for acceptance to work you need to switch your focus from result to the process. Accept that anxiety is an important part of a survival mechanism. Although sensations anxiety causes can be uncomfortable, reduction of anxiety level reduces intensity of these sensations. Remember, these are only feelings and thoughts. They can not hurt you.

It is very common to fear that removal of resistance will cause your anxiety to get worse. Seems logical enough, but as you already noticed, anxiety has little to do with logic. We do not get this result because the main thing feeding your anxiety was your worry and your fear.

Imagine anxiety as a river. You may imagine your resistance as a dam that stops you from being swept away when in fact your resistance is giving this river that immense power. Without this source of power it is just a peaceful stream which is going to flow by. If we continue with this metaphor, your resistance was a rickety dam that kept your anxiety at high levels and no matter how hard you tried it would regularly get swept away. Acceptance and invitation of anxiety removes this ineffectual dam thus reducing your anxiety level and eliminating panic attacks.

Acceptance of anxiety is not an easy thing to do, especially in the early stages but use improvement you feel as your motivator to move forward inch-by-inch until anxiety completely looses it's grip on you and you are the master of your fate again.

CHAPTER 8

SPECIFIC FEARS

Sometimes fear can take over our lives and stop us from doing what we want or need to do in order to improve and enjoy our lives. In addition to the program I would like to share with you this quick guide for dealing with the most common fears.

Eleanor Roosevelt said this about fear, *"You gain strength, courage, and confidence by every experience in which you really stop to look fear in the face. You are able to say to yourself, "I lived through this horror. I can take the next thing that comes along.""*

Year after year the list of the most common fears remains the same and if you suffer from fear of public speaking, flying or heights you are not alone. Fear of flying is in fact so common that 1 in 3 Americans suffer from some level of this fear.

Fears, like anxiety, are not rooted in an objective truth but are results of our irrational beliefs. This is why fear of public speaking ranks much higher than the fear of dying.

Below are quick guides that will reduce and eliminate fear from your life.

8.1. FEAR OF PUBLIC SPEAKING

Public speaking does not necessary mean standing on a podium and giving a speech. Public speaking comes in lots of different forms. Fear of public speaking may be standing in your way of achieving personal and professional goals.

Scott Adams shared these words of encouragement, *"We do not always have an accurate view of our own potential. I think most people who are frightened of public speaking and can not imagine they might feel different as a result of training. Do not assume you know how much potential you have. Sometimes the only way to know what you can do is to test yourself."*

You can remove this fear by following these 18 steps:

1. Be prepared - write your speech and think about details of your upcoming speech. Write a script that details everything from taking your position to walking away.

2. Practice - go over your speech and learn it. Do not try to learn it by hard. Prepare bullet points that will allow you to keep your speech on track.

3. Get into a flow - during your practice runs find a rhythm to your speech.

4. Focus on your breathing - coordinate your breathing with the rhythm of the speech. Use pauses that occur due to breathing as a tool to increase the impact of your speech.

5. Practice in front of the mirror - use a mirror to practice and improve your facial expressions, gestures, posture and movements.

6. Get to know your voice - during the speech you will be able to hear yourself and for most people hearing their own voice for the first time can be disorientating as it sounds nothing like you expect. Record your speech and listen to it. This will allow you to get used to the sound of your voice and to improve your speech.

7. Practice in front of people - ask someone you feel comfortable with to listen to your speech. This will build up your speaking experience and you will get valuable advice.

8. Practice some more - use any opportunity you get to speak in front of a group of people. If you have regular meetings at work with suggestions part, prepare and give a short speech with some sort of suggestion. To gain more

practice you can join your local public speaking class.

9. Exercise before the speech - if you ever watched comedy specials or recordings of live concerts you must have noticed one thing all performers did before going on stage - they all did a small exercise. You can do few jumping jacks, have a walk or do other exercise. This will loosen you up and it will burn a bit of that excess energy.

10. Prepare notes - to keep you on track you should have cards with speech key point prepared or you can use presentation tools for this purpose. You might not look at your notes once during the speech but just the knowledge that you have them will give you peace of mind. Have them just in case.

11. Eliminate fear of failure - go through concerns you have and eliminate them. For instance, you may be concerned that audience will be bored by your speech. To challenge this worry you

can point out to yourself that your speech has few very interesting facts and your audience is comprised of professionals who will benefit greatly from the information you are going to share with them.

12. Focus on your speech not the audience - focus on delivering speech and information you are sharing.

13. Be well informed about the subject - do an extensive research about the subject. Having this additional information allows you to speak with more certainty and will remove fear of additional questions.

14. Embrace the fear - this fear is what motivates you to practice one more time. Use this fear to improve and remember that even people who give hundreds of speeches still get this fear.

15. Staying out of focus - do not try to read reactions of the audience. Shift your gaze in a pattern which will have you

looking at every part of the audience without focusing on any one person.

16. Water - have a sip of water before giving a speech and always have water available during the speech. You can even integrate taking a sip of water during the speech to give it more drama or to emphasize a point.

17. Enjoy this experience - all these people are listening to you and most of them look up to you because you are able to speak in front of all these people. Take pride in this.

18. Constantly improve - use your experience from previous speech to improve your next one.

8.2. FEAR OF FLYING

Fear of flying is an extremely common one. This can be blamed on media coverage and on the lack of understanding of how planes function. Here are some tips that will help you next time to reach your destination without a burden of an additional baggage of anxiety.

1. Get informed - part of this fear stems from the lack of understanding or misunderstanding of flying. Watch some

documentaries to learn how planes, dispatch service and airports work to keep you safe. Learn about the extraordinary safety statistics of flying.

2. Create a detailed plan - for some people fear of flying starts with the airport entrance. No wonder as you have limited time to navigate this maze like structure. Use airport floor map to get acquainted with the route you will take to your gate. Prepare your documents and keep them in an order you will need them. Arrive at a time which will allow you to arrive at your gate with some time to spare.

3. Understand processes - security checks and requirement to show your documents can feel intrusive and can act as anxiety triggers. Use relaxation techniques and understand that these procedures are designed to keep you and everyone else safe.

4. Explore your fear - try to pin point what false belief your fear is based on.

This may result in a realization that none single aspect of flying actually scares you.

5. Visualization - day before the flight, go through your next day in your imagination. Start with the taxi picking you up and end up with exiting on your destination safe and sound.

6. Try virtual reality - use virtual reality device to play out the flight while still on the ground. The use of virtual reality for exposure therapy has been proven to be effective and very cost efficient.

7. Use breathing and muscle relaxation techniques - use techniques you learned in the second chapter to relax during the flight.

8. Enjoy this experience - get a seat next to the window so you can look outside. The view of earth from the birds eye view is astonishing, magnificent and can not be compared to anything else. It is truly humbling and will help you put everything in perspective.

Seeing how small we are will help you realize how insignificant are issues you bother yourself with.

Flying opens up the great big world that is waiting to be discovered by you.

8.3. FEAR OF HEIGHTS

Fear of heights can vary from a fluttering in the tummy, to a full on panic attack. Avoiding being exposed to heights is not an answer.

Here are seven tips that will help you get this fear under control:

1. Explore your fear - in many circumstances, the fear of falling from heights is completely unfounded. Examine what do you fear specifically.

2. Notice safety equipment - when you feel fear taking you over, apply breathing exercise and when initial fear has subsided tell yourself "look at all this safety equipment that protects me from falling." Notice barriers, rails and other equipment installed on the site to keep you safe.

3. Visualization - imagine being on the roof of a building or on the hill. Use virtual reality glasses to visit Empire State Building viewing deck and similar places.

4. Gradual exposure - in order to conquer my fear of heights I jumped with a parachute. If you feel that this is too drastic for you, start gradually. Start off by walking over to a window and looking down. Gradually increase height and decrease barriers.

5. Do not do it alone - open up about your fear to people you trust and employ their help to overcome this obstacle.

6. Use breathing exercise - if you feel that fear is overpowering you, stop and use breathing exercise to regain your composure.

7. Use thought restructuring - employ positive self-talk and questions to change your automatic response.

CONCLUSION

Self improvement is not a destination but a journey. Only through ongoing dedication and diligence you will ensure that you will be able to achieve and exceed your goals. Every great voyage starts with the first step and reading this book was your first all-important step towards anxiety free life. Implement these instructions and you are guaranteed to feel immense relief and improvement of your life quality.

Every single advice you received in this book will continue to bring you peace of mind, improve your health, improve your relationships and help you achieve your professional aspirations. Take this advice to heart and watch yourself grow. Everything is in your hands. You have the tools you require, now it is turn for the most important part - use them.

Imagine your life in a near future. Imagine encountering various situations and handling them in a cool, calm and collected way. Imagine how having peace of mind will improve your current relationships and help you build new ones.

Imagine how it will feel to be able to help others.

This is the future you deserve and this is the future which is waiting for you.

NOTES

NOTES

Made in the USA
Las Vegas, NV
13 August 2023